D0592522

For Esme, Clara and Toby,
who love Christmas

KEEP
CALM
AT
CHRISTMAS

KEEP CALM AT CHRISTMAS

GOOD ADVICE FOR CHRISTMAS TIME

EBURY
PRESS

7 9 10 8 6

This edition published 2011
First published in 2011 by Ebury Press, an imprint of Ebury Publishing
A Random House Group company

Copyright © Ebury Press 2011

The Random House Group Limited Reg. No. 954009

Addresses for companies within the Random House Group can be found at
www.randomhouse.co.uk

A CIP catalogue record for this book is available from the British Library

The Random House Group Limited supports The Forest Stewardship
Council (FSC®), the leading international forest certification organisation.
Our books carrying the FSC label are printed on FSC® certified paper.
FSC is the only forest certification scheme endorsed by the leading
environmental organisations, including Greenpeace. Our paper
procurement policy can be found at www.randomhouse.co.uk/environment

Designed and set by seagulls.net

Printed in Germany by GGP Media GmbH, Pössneck

ISBN 9780091945053

To buy books by your favourite authors and register for offers visit
www.randomhouse.co.uk

A CHRISTMAS GAMBOL OFT COULD CHEER THE POOR MAN'S HEART THROUGH HALF THE YEAR.

Sir Walter Scott

CONTENTS

The giving…
…And the receiving of gifts
Children
Friends and family
The turkey
Food
Drink
Overindulgence
Christmas TV
Goodwill to all men
Bah humbug
Comfort and joy
Religion
Spirit of Christmas
New Year

INTRODUCTION

Christmas comes but once a year, goes the old saying – even if it does now appear to begin in late September and carry on into the first weeks of the New Year. This early arrival and late departure, driven by the financial concerns of greedy merchants, is meat and drink to certain kind of curmudgeon. Despite their protests at the deplorable commercialisation of Christmas, they take secret joy in spotting its ever-earlier arrival, probably plotting the dates on a spreadsheet and exploring the correlations between the premature arrival of tinsel in the shops and the lack of back-bone in the nation's youth.

The traditional nativity scene, with the infant and mother centre stage surrounded by shepherds, wise men and lowing cattle (Joseph lurking at the back looking a bit embarrassed; turns out he's not even the real father), is still one that most of us recognise. Anyone acquainted with young children will have seen the Christmas story played out simply and movingly, often enhanced with supporting characters puzzlingly absent from the Gospels: talking mice, stable-dwelling lobsters and even Bethlehem-bound ninja turtles.

Somewhere in the tangle of Christmas lies its religious, dogmatic heart: do you follow the creed of Delia, Jamie or Gordon when it comes to cooking the turkey? Eating and drinking to excess, as demanded by convention, is a key element to a satisfactory Yule. Apart from Christmas morning, stag parties are the only other legitimate occasions when

it is considered good form to start drinking at break-
fast. Gorging throughout the day before descend-
ing into a food- and alcohol-induced coma around
late afternoon, from which one is roused in the time-
honoured custom of an invitation to play charades,
is the shape of Christmas for many.

But beneath the hype, the relentless merchan-
dising, the fake snow and the sound of Slade echo-
ing through every shopping centre in Britain, the
magic of Christmas is still there. Why else would
we put so much effort into getting it right, and be so
disappointed if it flops, if deep down we didn't still
have a splinter of the excitement and wonder of the
Christmases of childhood in our hearts? We still all
hope for the innocent pleasure of a white Christmas, just like the ones we probably never really
knew. We have an image of what the perfect Christmas should be like and we cleave to the idea, even

as we slope into the bookies for a bet on whether a snowflake will fall on the Met Office roof on the 25th December.

Nonetheless, it seems that whatever we throw at Christmas, it still comes through with its old magic and promise of a respite from the daily grind, and a time to appreciate the things that really matter. Like friends, family, and the *Morecambe and Wise Christmas Special*. So use the advice of this little tome to steel yourself for the stress-inducing marathon that awaits. Keep Calm and Merry Christmas.

CHRISTMAS

A MERRY CHRISTMAS TO EVERYBODY! A HAPPY NEW YEAR TO ALL THE WORLD!

Charles Dickens

I HEARD THE BELLS
ON CHRISTMAS DAY.
THEIR OLD FAMILIAR
CAROLS PLAY.
AND WILD AND
SWEET THE
WORDS REPEAT.
OF PEACE ON EARTH
GOODWILL TO MEN.

Henry Wadsworth Longfellow

CHRISTMAS IS A NECESSITY. THERE HAS TO BE AT LEAST ONE DAY OF THE YEAR TO REMIND US THAT WE'RE HERE FOR SOMETHING ELSE BESIDES OURSELVES.

Eric Sevareid

IT IS CHRISTMAS IN THE HEART THAT PUTS CHRISTMAS IN THE AIR.

W T Ellis

CHRISTMAS IS THE DAY THAT HOLDS ALL TIME TOGETHER.

Alexander Smith

HOLIDAYS

IT IS THE ONE
SEASON OF THE YEAR
WHEN WE CAN LAY
ASIDE ALL GNAWING
WORRY, INDULGE IN
SENTIMENT WITHOUT
CENSURE, ASSUME
THE CAREFREE FAITH
OF CHILDHOOD, AND
JUST PLAIN 'HAVE
FUN.' WHETHER THEY

CALL IT YULETIDE, NOEL, WEINACHTEN, OR CHRISTMAS, PEOPLE AROUND THE EARTH THIRST FOR ITS REFRESHMENT AS THE DESERT TRAVELLER FOR THE OASIS.

D D Monroe

I ONCE WANTED TO BECOME AN ATHEIST, BUT I GAVE UP — THEY HAVE NO HOLIDAYS.

Henry Youngman

NOTHING
SAYS HOLIDAYS,
LIKE A CHEESE LOG.

Ellen DeGeneres

PARTIES

CHRISTMAS IS A TIME
WHEN EVERYBODY
WANTS HIS PAST
FORGOTTEN AND HIS
PRESENT REMEMBERED.
WHAT I DON'T LIKE
ABOUT OFFICE
CHRISTMAS PARTIES
IS LOOKING FOR A
JOB THE NEXT DAY.

Phyllis Diller

AT EVERY PARTY THERE ARE TWO KINDS OF PEOPLE — THOSE WHO WANT TO GO HOME AND THOSE WHO DON'T. THE TROUBLE IS, THEY ARE USUALLY MARRIED TO EACH OTHER.

Ann Landers

HEAR NO EVIL, SPEAK NO EVIL — AND YOU'LL NEVER BE INVITED TO A PARTY.

Oscar Wilde

NEVER BE THE FIRST TO ARRIVE AT A PARTY OR THE LAST TO GO HOME, AND NEVER, EVER BE BOTH.

David Brown

A DOG IS FOR LIFE, NOT JUST FOR CHRISTMAS. SO BE CAREFUL AT THE OFFICE CHRISTMAS PARTY.

Jimmy Carr

AT THE OFFICE
PARTY YOU'RE
SUPPOSED TO SIT
NAKED ON TOP OF
THE PHOTOCOPIER,
NOT THE SHREDDER.

David Letterman

NO MAN DOES
RIGHT BY A WOMAN
AT A PARTY.

Harry Golden

SHOPPING

FROM A COMMERCIAL POINT OF VIEW, IF CHRISTMAS DID NOT EXIST IT WOULD BE NECESSARY TO INVENT IT.

Katharine Whitehorn

TO PERCEIVE CHRISTMAS THROUGH ITS WRAPPINGS BECOMES MORE DIFFICULT WITH EVERY YEAR.

E B White

ONCE AGAIN, WE
COME TO THE
HOLIDAY SEASON,
A DEEPLY RELIGIOUS
TIME THAT EACH OF
US OBSERVES, IN HIS
OWN WAY, BY GOING
TO THE MALL OF
HIS CHOICE.

Dave Barry

IF MEN LIKED SHOPPING, THEY'D CALL IT RESEARCH.

Cynthia Nelms

A CHRISTMAS SHOPPER'S COMPLAINT IS ONE OF LONG-STANDING.

Anon

EXPENSE

ABOUT ALL YOU CAN DO IS DREAM OF A WHITE CHRISTMAS, FOR IT SEEMS LIKE IT ALWAYS LEAVES MOST OF US IN THE RED.

Anon

**OH, FOR THE
GOOD OLD DAYS
WHEN PEOPLE
WOULD STOP
CHRISTMAS
SHOPPING WHEN
THEY RAN OUT
OF MONEY.**

Anon

CHRISTMAS IS THE
TIME WHEN KIDS TELL
SANTA WHAT THEY
WANT AND ADULTS
PAY FOR IT. DEFICITS
ARE WHEN ADULTS
TELL GOVERNMENT
WHAT THEY WANT
AND THEIR KIDS
PAY FOR IT.

Robert Lamm

THE CHRISTMAS SEASON HAS COME TO MEAN THE PERIOD WHEN THE PUBLIC PLAYS SANTA CLAUS TO THE MERCHANTS.

John Andrew Holmes

MANY BANKS HAVE A NEW KIND OF CHRISTMAS CLUB IN OPERATION. THE NEW CLUB HELPS YOU SAVE MONEY TO PAY FOR LAST YEAR'S GIFTS.

Anon

HOME FOR
CHRISTMAS

**FOR CENTURIES
MEN HAVE KEPT
AN APPOINTMENT
WITH CHRISTMAS.
CHRISTMAS MEANS
FELLOWSHIP,
FEASTING, GIVING
AND RECEIVING,
A TIME OF GOOD
CHEER, HOME.**

W J Ronald Tucker

AT CHRISTMAS, ALL ROADS LEAD HOME.

Marjorie Holmes

HAPPY, HAPPY CHRISTMAS, THAT CAN WIN US BACK TO THE DELUSIONS OF OUR CHILDHOOD DAYS, RECALL TO THE OLD MAN THE PLEASURES OF HIS YOUTH, AND TRANSPORT THE TRAVELLER BACK TO HIS OWN FIRESIDE AND QUIET HOME!

Charles Dickens

DECK THE
HALLS

NO MATTER HOW
CAREFULLY YOU
STORED THE LIGHTS
LAST YEAR, THEY
WILL BE SNARLED
AGAIN THIS
CHRISTMAS.

Robert Kirby

TINSEL IS REALLY
SNAKES' MIRRORS.

Steven Wright

NEVER WORRY ABOUT THE SIZE OF YOUR CHRISTMAS TREE. IN THE EYES OF CHILDREN, THEY ARE ALL 30 FEET TALL.

Larry Wilde

PERHAPS THE BEST YULETIDE DECORATION IS BEING WREATHED IN SMILES.

Anon

SNOW

A GREEN
CHRISTMAS
MAKES A FAT
CHURCHYARD.

English proverb

THE AGEING PROCESS HAS YOU FIRMLY IN ITS GRASP IF YOU NEVER GET THE URGE TO THROW A SNOWBALL.

Doug Larson

THE FIRST FALL OF SNOW IS NOT ONLY AN EVENT, IT IS A MAGICAL EVENT. YOU GO TO BED IN ONE KIND OF A WORLD AND WAKE UP IN ANOTHER QUITE DIFFERENT, AND IF THIS IS NOT ENCHANTMENT THEN WHERE IS IT TO BE FOUND?

J B Priestley

THERE'S ONE GOOD THING ABOUT SNOW, IT MAKES YOUR LAWN LOOK AS NICE AS YOUR NEIGHBOUR'S.

Clyde Moore

CHRISTMAS
EVE

THERE ARE NO STRANGERS ON CHRISTMAS EVE.

George Melton (Harry Carey)
in 'Beyond Tomorow'

IT'S CHRISTMAS EVE. IT'S THE ONE NIGHT OF THE YEAR WHEN WE ALL ACT A LITTLE NICER, WE SMILE A LITTLE EASIER, WE CHEER A LITTLE MORE. FOR A COUPLE OF HOURS OUT OF THE WHOLE YEAR WE ARE THE PEOPLE THAT WE ALWAYS HOPED WE WOULD BE.

Frank Cross (Bill Murray) in 'Scrooged'

LET'S BE NAUGHTY AND SAVE SANTA THE TRIP.

Gary Allen

SANTA

THE MAIN REASON SANTA IS SO JOLLY IS BECAUSE HE KNOWS WHERE ALL THE BAD GIRLS LIVE.

George Carlin

YOU KNOW YOU'RE GETTING OLD, WHEN SANTA STARTS LOOKING YOUNGER.

Robert Paul

WHY IS CHRISTMAS JUST LIKE A DAY AT THE OFFICE? YOU DO ALL THE WORK AND THE FAT GUY WITH THE SUIT GETS ALL THE CREDIT.

Anon

THERE ARE THREE STAGES OF MAN: HE BELIEVES IN SANTA CLAUS; HE DOES NOT BELIEVE IN SANTA CLAUS; HE IS SANTA CLAUS.

Bob Phillips

WHAT DO YOU CALL PEOPLE WHO ARE AFRAID OF SANTA CLAUS? CLAUSTROPHOBIC.

Anon

THE GIVING...

NOTHING'S AS MEAN AS GIVING A LITTLE CHILD SOMETHING USEFUL FOR CHRISTMAS.

Kin Hubbard

WE SHOULD GIVE AS
WE WOULD RECEIVE,
CHEERFULLY,
QUICKLY, AND
WITHOUT
HESITATION; FOR
THERE IS NO GRACE
IN A BENEFIT THAT
STICKS TO THE
FINGERS.

Seneca

GUILT: THE GIFT THAT KEEPS ON GIVING.

Erma Bombeck

MAIL YOUR PACKAGES EARLY SO THE POST OFFICE CAN LOSE THEM IN TIME FOR CHRISTMAS.

Johnny Carson

EVERY GIFT WHICH IS GIVEN, EVEN THOUGH IT BE SMALL, IS IN REALITY GREAT, IF IT IS GIVEN WITH AFFECTION.

Pindar

ANYONE WHO BELIEVES THAT MEN ARE THE EQUAL OF WOMEN HAS NEVER SEEN A MAN TRYING TO WRAP A CHRISTMAS PRESENT.

Anon

PRESENTS ARE THE BEST WAY TO SHOW SOMEONE HOW MUCH YOU CARE. IT IS LIKE THIS TANGIBLE THING THAT YOU CAN POINT TO AND SAY 'HEY MAN, I LOVE YOU THIS MANY DOLLARS WORTH.'

Michael Scott (Steve Carell) in 'The Office'

...AND THE RECEIVING OF GIFTS

THE ONE THING WOMEN DON'T WANT TO FIND IN THEIR STOCKINGS ON CHRISTMAS MORNING IS THEIR HUSBAND.

Joan Rivers

IN SUGGESTING GIFTS: MONEY IS APPROPRIATE, AND ONE SIZE FITS ALL.

William Randolph Hearst

PRESENTS, I OFTEN SAY, ENDEAR ABSENTS.

Charles Lamb

CHILDREN

THERE'S NOTHING SADDER IN THIS WORLD THAN TO AWAKE CHRISTMAS MORNING AND NOT BE A CHILD.

Erma Bombeck

CHRISTMAS TO A CHILD IS THE FIRST TERRIBLE PROOF THAT TO TRAVEL HOPEFULLY IS BETTER THAN TO ARRIVE.

Stephen Fry

NO SELF-RESPECTING MOTHER WOULD RUN OUT OF INTIMIDATIONS ON THE EVE OF A MAJOR HOLIDAY.

Erma Bombeck

THREE PHRASES THAT SUM UP CHRISTMAS ARE: PEACE ON EARTH, GOODWILL TO MEN, AND BATTERIES NOT INCLUDED.

Anon

A CHILD THAT'S BORN ON A CHRISTMAS DAY, IS FAIR AND WISE, GOOD AND GAY.

English proverb

FRIENDS
AND FAMILY

VISITS ALWAYS GIVE PLEASURE — IF NOT THE ARRIVAL, THE DEPARTURE.

Portuguese proverb

**SANTA CLAUS HAS
THE RIGHT IDEA —
VISIT PEOPLE ONLY
ONCE A YEAR.**

Victor Borge

**WHEN OUR
RELATIVES ARE AT
HOME, WE HAVE TO
THINK OF ALL THEIR
GOOD POINTS OR
IT WOULD BE
IMPOSSIBLE TO
ENDURE THEM.**

George Bernard Shaw

HAPPINESS IS HAVING A LARGE, LOVING, CARING, CLOSE-KNIT FAMILY IN ANOTHER CITY.

George Burns

FISH AND VISITORS SMELL IN THREE DAYS.

Benjamin Franklin

FAMILIES ARE LIKE FUDGE — MOSTLY SWEET WITH A FEW NUTS.

Anon

IF YOU CANNOT GET RID OF THE FAMILY SKELETON, YOU MAY AS WELL MAKE IT DANCE.

George Bernard Shaw

PEOPLE REALLY ACT WEIRD AT CHRISTMAS TIME! WHAT OTHER TIME OF YEAR DO YOU SIT IN FRONT OF A DEAD TREE IN THE LIVING ROOM AND EAT NUTS AND SWEETS OUT OF YOUR SOCKS?

Anon

THE TURKEY

A TURKEY NEVER VOTED FOR AN EARLY CHRISTMAS.

Irish proverb

MOST TURKEYS TASTE BETTER THE DAY AFTER; MY MOTHER'S TASTED BETTER THE DAY BEFORE.

Rita Rudner

FOOD

**CHRISTMAS ITSELF
MAY BE CALLED
INTO QUESTION, IF
CARRIED SO FAR
IT CREATES
INDIGESTION.**

Ralph Bergengren

THE WORST GIFT IS A FRUITCAKE. THERE IS ONLY ONE FRUITCAKE IN THE ENTIRE WORLD, AND PEOPLE KEEP SENDING IT TO EACH OTHER.

Johnny Carson

I TRUST CHRISTMAS BRINGS TO YOU ITS TRADITIONAL MIX OF GOOD FOOD AND VIOLENT STOMACH CRAMPS.

Ebenezer Blackadder (Rowan Atkinson)
in 'Blackadder's Christmas Carol'

EAT AND DRINK ON CHRISTMAS — FOR EASTER, NEW CLOTHING.

Irish proverb

DRINK

THE PROPER BEHAVIOUR ALL THROUGH THE HOLIDAY SEASON IS TO BE DRUNK. THIS DRUNKENNESS CULMINATES ON NEW YEAR'S EVE, WHEN YOU GET SO DRUNK YOU KISS THE PERSON YOU'RE MARRIED TO.

P J O'Rourke

DO NOT ALLOW CHILDREN TO MIX DRINKS. IT IS UNSEEMLY AND THEY USE TOO MUCH VERMOUTH.

Steve Allen

SOMETIMES TOO MUCH TO DRINK IS BARELY ENOUGH.

Mark Twain

THERE'S NOTHING LIKE A COLD BEER ON A HOT CHRISTMAS MORNING.

Homer Simpson

OVER-INDULGENCE

PEOPLE ARE SO WORRIED ABOUT WHAT THEY EAT BETWEEN CHRISTMAS AND THE NEW YEAR, BUT THEY REALLY SHOULD BE WORRIED ABOUT WHAT THEY EAT BETWEEN THE NEW YEAR AND CHRISTMAS.

Anon

DYSPEPSIA IS THE REMORSE OF A GUILTY STOMACH.

A Kerr

IF YOUR STOMACH DISPUTES YOU, LIE DOWN AND PACIFY IT WITH COOL THOUGHTS.

Satchel Paige

EAT, DRINK, AND BE MERRY, FOR TOMORROW YE DIET.

William Gilmore Beymer

CHRISTMAS TV

OH LOOK, YET ANOTHER CHRISTMAS TV SPECIAL! HOW TOUCHING TO HAVE THE MEANING OF CHRISTMAS BROUGHT TO US BY COLA, FAST FOOD, AND BEER... WHO'D HAVE EVER

GUESSED THAT PRODUCT CONSUMPTION, POPULAR ENTERTAINMENT, AND SPIRITUALITY WOULD MIX SO HARMONIOUSLY?

Calvin and Hobbes

IF GOD HAD MEANT CHRISTMAS TO BE A FAMILY OCCASION HE WOULDN'T HAVE INVENTED TV, WOULD HE?

Rory McGrath

GOODWILL
TO ALL MEN

CHRISTMAS IS THE SEASON FOR KINDLING THE FIRE OF HOSPITALITY IN THE HALL, THE GENIAL FLAME OF CHARITY IN THE HEART.

Washington Irving

IF YOU HAVEN'T GOT ANY CHARITY IN YOUR HEART, YOU HAVE THE WORST KIND OF HEART TROUBLE.

Bob Hope

REMEMBER, IF CHRISTMAS ISN'T FOUND IN YOUR HEART, YOU WON'T FIND IT UNDER A TREE.

Charlotte Carpenter

I WISH WE COULD PUT UP SOME OF THE CHRISTMAS SPIRIT IN JARS AND OPEN A JAR OF IT EVERY MONTH.

Harlan Miller

ONE OF THE NICE THINGS ABOUT CHRISTMAS IS THAT YOU CAN MAKE PEOPLE FORGET THE PAST WITH A PRESENT.

Anon

CHRISTMAS GIFT SUGGESTIONS: TO YOUR ENEMY, FORGIVENESS. TO AN OPPONENT, TOLERANCE. TO A FRIEND, YOUR HEART. TO A CUSTOMER, SERVICE. TO ALL, CHARITY. TO EVERY CHILD, A GOOD EXAMPLE. TO YOURSELF, RESPECT.

Oren Arnold

UNLESS WE MAKE CHRISTMAS AN OCCASION TO SHARE OUR BLESSINGS, ALL THE SNOW IN ALASKA WON'T MAKE IT 'WHITE'.

Bing Crosby

CHRISTMAS IS NOT A TIME NOR A SEASON, BUT A STATE OF MIND. TO CHERISH PEACE AND GOODWILL, TO BE PLENTEOUS IN MERCY, IS TO HAVE THE REAL SPIRIT OF CHRISTMAS.

Calvin Coolidge

BAH
HUMBUG

CHRISTMAS IS A TIME WHEN YOU GET HOMESICK — EVEN WHEN YOU'RE HOME.

Carol Nelson

'A MERRY CHRISTMAS,
UNCLE! GOD SAVE
YOU!' CRIED A
CHEERFUL VOICE.
'BAH' SAID SCROOGE.
'HUMBUG!'

Charles Dickens

A SEVERED FOOT IS THE PERFECT STOCKING STUFFER.

Mitch Hedberg

MERRY CHRISTMAS,
NEARLY EVERYBODY!

Ogden Nash

BLAST THIS CHRISTMAS MUSIC. IT'S JOYFUL AND TRIUMPHANT.

Grinch (Jim Carrey) in
'How the Grinch Stole Christmas'

BAH! HOW HOLLOW IT ALL IS! ALWAYS ON CHRISTMAS, THOUGH, I FEEL MY OWN HEART SOFTEN— TOWARD THE LATE JUDAS ISCARIOT.

Ambrose Bierce

COMFORT
AND JOY

A LOVELY THING ABOUT CHRISTMAS IS THAT IT'S COMPULSORY, LIKE A THUNDERSTORM, AND WE ALL GO THROUGH IT TOGETHER.

Garrison Keillor

AT CHRISTMAS PLAY AND MAKE GOOD CHEER, FOR CHRISTMAS COMES BUT ONCE A YEAR.

Thomas Tusser

GIFTS OF TIME AND LOVE ARE SURELY THE BASIC INGREDIENTS OF A TRULY MERRY CHRISTMAS.

Peg Bracken

CHRISTMAS IS A BRIDGE. WE NEED BRIDGES AS THE RIVER OF TIME FLOWS PAST. TODAY'S CHRISTMAS SHOULD MEAN CREATING HAPPY HOURS FOR TOMORROW AND RELIVING THOSE OF YESTERDAY.

Gladys Taber

RELIGION

HOW MANY OBSERVE CHRIST'S BIRTHDAY! HOW FEW, HIS PRECEPTS! O! 'TIS EASIER TO KEEP HOLIDAYS THAN COMMANDMENTS.

Benjamin Franklin

WHEN WE WERE
CHILDREN WE WERE
GRATEFUL TO THOSE
WHO FILLED OUR
STOCKINGS AT
CHRISTMAS TIME. WHY
ARE WE NOT GRATEFUL
TO GOD FOR FILLING
OUR STOCKINGS
WITH LEGS?

G K Chesterton

THIS IS THE MESSAGE OF CHRISTMAS: WE ARE NEVER ALONE.

Taylor Caldwell

THE CHRISTMAS TREE HAS TAKEN THE PLACE OF THE ALTAR IN TOO MUCH OF OUR MODERN CHRISTMAS OBSERVANCE.

Anon

CHRISTMAS WAVES A MAGIC WAND OVER THIS WORLD, AND BEHOLD, EVERYTHING IS SOFTER AND MORE BEAUTIFUL.

Norman Vincent Peale

ROSES ARE REDDISH
VIOLETS ARE BLUISH
IF IT WEREN'T FOR
CHRISTMAS
WE'D ALL BE JEWISH.

Benny Hill

SPIRIT OF CHRISTMAS

NEXT TO A CIRCUS THERE AIN'T NOTHING THAT PACKS UP AND TEARS OUT FASTER THAN THE CHRISTMAS SPIRIT.

Kin Hubbard

CHRISTMAS IS NOT AS MUCH ABOUT OPENING OUR PRESENTS AS OPENING OUR HEARTS.

Janice Maeditere

THERE IS NO IDEAL CHRISTMAS; ONLY THE ONE CHRISTMAS YOU DECIDE TO MAKE AS A REFLECTION OF YOUR VALUES, DESIRES, AFFECTIONS, TRADITIONS.

Bill McKibben

MAY WE NOT 'SPEND' CHRISTMAS OR 'OBSERVE' CHRISTMAS, BUT RATHER 'KEEP' IT.

Peter Marshall

AT CHRISTMAS I NO
MORE DESIRE A
ROSE, THAN WISH
A SNOW IN MAY'S
NEW-FANGLED
SHOWS; BUT LIKE OF
EACH THING THAT IN
SEASON GROWS.

William Shakespeare

THERE MUST BE SOMETHING GHOSTLY IN THE AIR OF CHRISTMAS—SOMETHING ABOUT THE CLOSE, MUGGY ATMOSPHERE THAT DRAWS UP THE GHOSTS, LIKE THE DAMPNESS OF THE SUMMER RAINS BRINGS OUT THE FROGS AND SNAILS.

Jerome K Jerome

NEW YEAR

NEW YEAR'S IS A
HARMLESS ANNUAL
INSTITUTION, OF NO
PARTICULAR USE TO
ANYBODY SAVE AS
A SCAPEGOAT FOR
PROMISCUOUS DRUNKS,
AND FRIENDLY CALLS
AND HUMBUG
RESOLUTIONS.

Mark Twain

MAY ALL YOUR TROUBLES LAST AS LONG AS YOUR NEW YEAR'S RESOLUTIONS.

Joey Adams

GOOD RESOLUTIONS ARE SIMPLY CHECKS THAT MEN DRAW ON A BANK WHERE THEY HAVE NO ACCOUNT.

Oscar Wilde

NEW YEAR'S EVE, WHERE AULD ACQUAINTANCE BE FORGOT. UNLESS, OF COURSE, THOSE TESTS COME BACK POSITIVE.

Jay Leno

**NEW YEAR'S DAY...
NOW IS THE
ACCEPTED TIME
TO MAKE YOUR
REGULAR ANNUAL
GOOD RESOLUTIONS.
NEXT WEEK YOU CAN
BEGIN PAVING HELL
WITH THEM AS
USUAL.**

Mark Twain

YOUTH IS WHEN YOU'RE ALLOWED TO STAY UP LATE ON NEW YEAR'S EVE. MIDDLE AGE IS WHEN YOU'RE FORCED TO.

Bill Vaughan

RING OUT THE OLD, RING IN THE NEW, RING, HAPPY BELLS, ACROSS THE SNOW: THE YEAR IS GOING, LET HIM GO; RING OUT THE FALSE, RING IN THE TRUE.

Alfred Lord Tennyson

MORE HELP IS AT HAND...